MARRIAGE MEDITATIONS

— **31 DAYS** —

A REMARKABLE MEDITATION BETWEEN HUSBAND AND WIFE

MARRIAGE MEDITATIONS

A Deeper Journey

CHRISTINE & CRAIG WESTHOFF

Scripture quotations taken from the (NASB®) New American Standard Bible®, Copyright © 1960, 1971, 1977, 1995, 2020 by The Lockman Foundation. Used by permission. All rights reserved. lockman.org

Scripture quotations marked (MSG) are taken from The Message, copyright © 1993, 2002, 2018 by Eugene H. Peterson. Used by permission of NavPress. . All rights reserved. Represented by Tyndale House Publishers.

Scripture quotations marked (NLT) are taken from the Holy Bible, New Living Translation, copyright ©1996, 2004, 2015 by Tyndale House Foundation. Used by permission of Tyndale House Publishers, Carol Stream, Illinois 60188.

Unless otherwise indicated, all Scripture quotations are from The ESV® Bible (The Holy Bible, English Standard Version®), copyright © 2001 by Crossway, a publishing ministry of Good News Publishers. Used by permission. All rights reserved.

Scripture quotations marked (NIV) are taken from the Holy Bible, New International Version®, NIV®. Copyright © 1973, 1978, 1984, 2011 by Biblica, Inc.™ Used by permission of Zondervan. All rights reserved worldwide. www.zondervan.comThe "NIV" and "New International Version" are trademarks registered in the United States Patent and Trademark Office by Biblica, Inc.™

Scripture quotations marked TPT are from The Passion Translation®. Copyright © 2017, 2018, 2020 by Passion & Fire Ministries, Inc. Used by permission. All rights reserved. ThePassionTranslation.com.

All rights reserved.

ISBN (paperback): 978-0-9965621-3-3
ISBN (hardcover): 978-0-9965621-4-0

Cover design and layout by Albatross Book Co.
Cover art by Abi Westhoff

Published by:
Hawkeye Press, a division of Hawkeye.Pro, LLC
hawkeye.pro

For Hugh & Kristen, Sam & Abi. Your marriages reflect the heart of Christ into a longing world. We love you more than you'll ever know, Love Mom and Dad

DAY 1

CHRISTINE

I was in prayer one day asking the Holy Spirit to help me love Jesus well.

Instantly, I saw the face of my husband.

I went back into prayer and asked God to teach me how to grow in my love for the Lord. And I saw the face of my husband.

I went back into prayer and tried to worship the One who sits on the throne. Once again, my husband's face appeared before me.

Finally, I stopped and listened. "Lord, what are you trying to say to me?"

"Loving your husband is your tutorial."

Please explain.

"As you learn to stand before your husband with an open heart, your heart will learn to stand before me with an open heart.

As you learn to give yourself fully to your husband, your heart will learn how to give yourself fully to me.

As you learn to receive the love of your husband, your heart will learn how to receive My Love.

As you let yourself be seen by him, as you learn how to lay down your pride before him, as you learn how to remain vulnerable with him, to radically trust him, to open your eyes and see beyond the surface of him, your heart will learn to do that with me."

And on and on it went. Intimacy with my husband is my training ground for intimacy with God Himself.

> "If someone says, 'I love God,' and hates his brother, he is a liar; for the one who does not love his brother whom he has seen, cannot love God whom he has not seen."
> (1 John 4:20, NASB)

Learning to love and be loved could take a lifetime. It may be excruciating. It may be glorious. It will absolutely be transformative. So, when my heart feels lazy and would rather not pursue, I'm motivated to draw near. When the ground is unsteady and my soul wants to hide, I rise again instead—and show up. I will steward my heart most of all and learn how to love my husband thoroughly. If I can do anything in this life well, may this be my most passionate aim.

> [if I] have not love, I am nothing."
> (1 Corinthians 13:2, ESV)

CRAIG

We all want to be understood.

Even God wants to be understood.

> *"And we know that the Son of God has come, and he has given us understanding so that we can know the true God."* 1 John 5:20(NLT)

The desire to be understood is quite normal.

But demanding it, complaining about it, trying to force it into being, simply prevents it from happening.

So we want something that we can't make happen. And often, the more we try, the more misunderstood we become. Which leaves us in a conundrum. This might sound weird but

Just stop.

Stop trying to be understood by your spouse.

Instead, make it your goal to understand.

I've found that as you seek to understand your wife, oftentimes you will be understood.

When you seek her, you actually position your heart to love well.

Because it stops being about you.

And your pursuit will draw you into fascination and curiosity all over again. As you seek to understand, your aim is to *know* her; not judge her. Just simply know and understand the essence of who she is.

Seeking to understand can mean asking all kinds of questions from fun and goofy, to serious and provocative; asking 'why' a lot, saying, "Don't stop. Tell me more."

When my wife does or says something that rubs me the wrong way, when she says something I disagree with or it simply confuses me, it's *always* an invitation to seek to understand her.

When my wife is struggling, fighting, feeling low, celebrating, joyful or peaceful,

Each moment is like an underwater cave I've discovered in a deep-sea excursion.

The cave reveals its secrets to the one who enters.

To know her, I must enter the mystery. To love her, I must enter the pursuit.

So breathe deeply and dive in!

In seeking to understand your wife, you pull out of a self-centered pursuit, and you find yourself chasing down selfless love.

And that, my friend, will often intrigue the other to want to understand you.

DAY 3

CHRISTINE

Sometimes, I need to step back and gaze. Gaze upon his heart, his mind, his view of the world. As I step back and simply watch him, I remember he's an individual. Unique and wonderful; strange and complicated. But oh so very loved by God. Just as he is. Just as he used to be, and as he will always be.

Aside from the One who made him, I'm his only true witness. The only one who will watch him live his life, walk his path, fight his fight. I'm a primary witness of his life. Then I step back and remember, I do not want him made in my image. I fell in love with this individual.

This man... flawed and perfect. Passionate, complicated, and simple. Intricate, guilty, and pure.

Sometimes, I need to climb inside of his skin and see how he sees, sense his atmosphere, experience his world. And remember that I will not be the one he answers to.

But I *will* answer for how I loved him. His life is lived before me, his heart is laid bare in front of me.

The least I could do is to spend my life trying to know him,
To truly see him, to treasure him.

DAY 4

CRAIG

I invite you to see your marriage as a calling; a gift that's been given to you.

> "God gives the gift of the single life to some, the gift of married life to others." (1 Corinthians 7:7, MSG)

God has seen fit to actually give you the grace to be married just as He has given others the grace to be single. This means when you married you entered into a vocation.

You said 'yes' to a strong impulse to follow a particular path. That's a calling.

If you've ever wondered what your calling is, and you find yourself married, well, you've discovered at least one major calling on your life.

Sure there are more, but we can sometimes think and act like our marriage is in the way of our calling. This is just not true, and agreeing with this lie can create a wake of rejection for your spouse.

Since God graced you with the calling to be married, what happens to all the other callings you sense in your heart?

Maybe we can see it this way: God knew about all the other delightful plans and callings on your life (they're His ideas) and He foresaw that your best environment to learn and grow in those other vocations would be through a primary vocation and strong impulse that you flung yourself into – marriage.

It is in fulfilling our most precious and profound calling as a spouse that we will see other callings fulfilled in our lives. All your other callings are sandwiched between what you wake up to and what you go to bed to — your spouse, your gift, your grace, your precious and beautiful calling.

DAY 5

CHRISTINE

I've seen marriages, over and over again, start deep and gradually, ever so slowly, rise to the surface of their own soul, and the surface of their spouse's soul.

For some reason they stop diving deep into each other's heart. Somewhere along the way, they stopped peering deeply into the other.

Somehow they lose the vision of intimate connection. They let go of the will, the courage, the energy it takes to stay in deep waters together. And in that fumble, they lose each other.

Somewhere they become indifferent to the dream to truly know and be known.

I wonder if it's the pain. Most marriages, I would venture to guess, start in the deep: love, hope, passion, and dreams. Lots and lots of dreams.

Two innocents in love with hearts wide open. Diving deeply into each other's souls every day, cherishing each other, in awe of the other.

Then comes the pain. It doesn't really matter what causes it. It always happens. People are flawed. Love is vulnerable. Pain happens. Always.

These are the moments of great choice. Do we keep our hearts open in the pain? After the pain? Do we hold fast to the courage it takes to deep-sea dive with this new information? Do we trust again, now that we're bruised? Do we keep our hearts open to be known, now that our safety isn't guaranteed?

It's a profound choice to give your heart to someone after you've awakened to their brokenness.

This is where the high-ask of covenant begins to bear its fruit.

This is the great battle ground. The fight for deep waters means I must fight my own instinct to self-protect and remain his and he remain mine. Open, willing, determined to stay deep. Forever. No matter what the cost. These are the decisions that make great marriages and we make them because Jesus made the same choice. For us. Over and over again.

CRAIG

It only seems right that I would view my marriage as a garden. A beautiful, lush, fruitful garden teeming with life with my wife and me right at the center of it.

As the husband, I have two primary goals in my mind all the time: to cultivate and keep.

> *"Then the Lord God took the man and put him into the garden of Eden to cultivate it and keep it."*
> (Genesis 2:15, NASB)

Eve was created from the rib of man while in the garden.

Cultivate and keep means to work for another, to guard, keep watch, protect.

That means my role, my calling, is to cultivate and keep this garden, this home, this woman who has entrusted her life to me, this marriage, this sacred space.

I will guard it, keep watch, and protect this union at all times. And I'm doing this work for another — my wife.

I often wonder what would have happened if Adam caught that devious little serpent, preventing it from ever coming in proximity of their special place, their oh-so-special union with each other and with God.

What I'm really talking about here is awareness. Can I remain aware enough, focused enough, to cultivate and keep this garden?

And can I remain aware of *myself?*

To cultivate and keep requires an awareness and watchfulness over what *we* are allowing into our home through our very own thoughts, words, deeds, attitudes and presence. I confess that I've occasionally released a serpent into my marriage due to self-centeredness and carelessness due to a lack of awareness. Alertness. Mindfulness. Attentiveness.

But it doesn't have to be that way. Let's be aware.

Eden means pleasure. So let's cultivate and keep our marriages in such a way that they remain gardens of pleasure! Where we hear the voice of the Lord walking ever so clearly, and the temptations of the serpent never make it past the gate. Work. Serve. Guard. Keep watch. Protect. Observe.

And ENJOY!!!

DAY 1

CHRISTINE

Oneness.

The scripture is clear. From the beginning to the end, God's passionate desire is intimate, intertwined, deep oneness with humans.

He longs for *such* union, *such* connection, that He had to demonstrate His heart through man and woman. He was compelled to create a sign; to artfully paint the picture for all to see and experience. Out of God's own intention for profound intimacy with you and me, out of His longing for oneness with mankind, He created the first human love, the first marriage. Listen to these first words of Adam about his wife!

> *"This is now bone of my bones and flesh of my flesh; she shall be called 'woman,' for she was taken out of man. That is why a man leaves his father and mother and is united to his wife, and they become one flesh."*
> (Genesis 2:23-25, NIV)

Oneness. She was taken out of man, Then made one flesh with man again.

Separate, yet one. Individual, yet intertwined. She was pulled out of Adam's very being, sculpted as an original, then invited to be one flesh again.

We were created from God's own hand, "Before I formed you in the womb, I knew you." Sculpted as individuals, then invited to be one with God through Christ.

One with Him again.

> *"For your Maker is your husband, the LORD of hosts is his name..."* (Isaiah 54:5, ESV)

My marriage is a sign to the world. A revelation to mankind of the love of a Creator and His longing for intimate union with mankind.

My marriage is a sign to the world of the ardent, amorous pursuit of God.

My marriage is one of the greatest prophetic words of all time.

This revelation will change you. It will alter how you live your life, how you love your husband, how you treat your marriage.

This revelation will set aflame your relationship with the Lord. It will unveil His ways, His purposes, His passions. It will take hold of you; possess you and set you on a pilgrimage of a different kind of love. A revelation of Heaven kind of love. An incarnational kind of love.

"For this reason, a man shall leave his father and mother and shall be joined to his wife, and the two shall become one flesh. This mystery is great; but I am speaking with reference to Christ and the church."
(Ephesians 5:31-32, NASB)

CRAIG

Most guys like to fix things. And, whether we realize it or not, oftentimes we try to fix our wives. She begins to share her heart with me and "Super Craig" immediately goes into fix it mode. I've done that often.

Then one day my exasperated wife said something incredibly profound to me. "Stop it. Please." I've learned that she really doesn't come to me for her or her circumstance to be fixed. She comes to me first and foremost to be seen, known, and heard.

"Fixing" is often rushing in with an answer before you've heard her heart.

She wants partnership in the pain. She wants understanding, safety and companionship in the confusion.

She wants presence. My presence that's packed with God's presence.

There is nothing the nearness of Christ cannot overcome. The nearness of Christ — not the nearness of Super Craig.

So, when you find your wife sharing what you would deem as a "fix it" situation, when you feel your "Superman" rising to the surface, stop. Breathe. And see it as a presence situation.

I dare say that nearly all "fix it" situations are actually an invitation into a holy moment; an intimate moment.

Where instead of *doing* for your wife, you get to *be* for your wife.

It's so simple that we often miss its power. And because it's wrapped up in essence instead of a perceivable productivity, we men can easily miss the point.

It's in being still that we make room for the Holy Spirit. He did create in the void, and he's still creating in the void.

So, if we can simply be present for our wives, she may end up feeling more loved, more seen, more known.

And in the void of the moment, in our listening, in our patience, God can create something new once again and say, "Let there be light."

DAY 9

CHRISTINE

I didn't think I was a judgmental person. That probably sounds arrogant, I know. But I honestly tried diligently to watch my words and accept people as they were.

Then one day the Lord whispered in my ear. The room began to spin, and my self deception came to a screeching halt. He gently, yet oh so firmly, spoke, "You don't have the right to even form an opinion about another human being."

He was reaching down deep into my soul; the place where I hid all the "shoulds," "ought-tos," and exasperations. Every conclusion I drew, every arrogant 'told you so' that stewed beneath the surface did not escape the watchful eye of my Father.

As I began to surrender my opinions, I realized that many of them were about my husband. You see, he had been clinically depressed for a few years at this point, and I felt tired. I thought I knew so much. I believed I knew what he needed to do. Hundreds of times I thought, "if he would only..." I stood at a distance with my judgments and my love was slowly growing cold.

On this day, the Lord removed the veil, and I saw. I saw my own soul in all its filth. I saw my own heart drenched in pride. I saw, and I trembled. What if Jesus loved me, as I had been loving my man? I began to repent. I released my conclusions, I rejected my opinions, and turned away from wanting to be right, for the sake of love. I once again put my husband back in the hands of the One who created his heart and soul.

The burden to fix, to heal, to alter my husband's life was back in its proper place— solely in the hands of the Master.

My call was to learn to love the love of my life. My invitation was to enter the classroom of unconditional love. The Lord reminded me, once again, that I am just as broken as the rest. To learn to love this broken man in sickness and in health was my journey of transformation.

To love the broken, there can be no fixing. To love the hurting, there can be no judgment. To love this man for the rest of my life, my opinions must die.

For God so loves the broken.
For God so loves me in my mess.
For God so loves my man.

CRAIG

I met them at a restaurant, Charlotte and Ken. They had been married 69 years! My wife and I were sitting across from each other celebrating our 27th anniversary and they were to my right... not sitting across from each other, but...

Next to each other. On the same side of the table... side by side.

They looked so satisfied. They didn't say much to each other.

They just sat next to each other...side by side.

My wife and I were enamored.

If you were paying attention you could feel the security they had in each other; in their history. You could sense the love that had grown deep, thick roots through the decades.

You could see the assurance that unity brings.

The quiet, beautiful strength that two vines have when they become intertwined.

It was a captivating side-by-side moment.

All the while, my wife and I were enjoying a face-to-face moment.

Staring into each other's eyes, reading each other's gaze. Remembering. Hoping. Flirting. Beckoning. Welcoming.

At one table a face-to-face moment; at the other table a side-by-side moment. Both are equally powerful, important and absolutely necessary.

"Side-by-Side" proclaims, "I'm here. I'm *for* you, and I'll never leave you. I've got your back. I like you. I enjoy being with you. My hand is yours. You are completely enough for me. Let's do this together."

"Face-to-Face" proclaims, "You're my beloved! I adore you. You slay me. I am captivated by your presence. I want you. My heart is yours. I long for you. Let's run away together…again!"

"Face-to-Face" and "Side-by-Side" partner with each other, pouring into each other, increasing the vitality of the other.

Make time for both.

They bring balance — equilibrium — and both are absolutely necessary.

DAY 11

CHRISTINE

> *"Above all, love each other deeply, because love covers over a multitude of sins."* (1 Peter 4:8, NIV)

Love covers.

Does *my* love cover? It's an honest question.

Marriage has to be *the* most vulnerable thing in the world to truly engage with. In the early years, my husband was a mysterious superhero that I believed was beyond perfect in every way, and I was demure, shy and utterly charming.

I can hardly write that without laughing out loud.

Over three decades later *none* of those oh-so-untrue images exist in our minds, and I'm deeply grateful.

Over the years our multi-layered, muddied brokenness just keeps revealing itself. Over and over again. He knows my dark places and I know his. He can sense when I'm off just by how I walk into a room, and I can see the look in his eye and know a storm is brewing, without saying a word.

You *will* know each other's most vulnerable, most fragile, most injured parts. You *will* see each other's dark spots, bruised places, fleshly ickys and sinful tendencies.

I remember the first argument we ever had. We had only been together a couple of months. My brother was over, and Craig said something (I don't even remember what it was) but I do remember that I thought he was wrong. I sharply corrected him in a demeaning fashion in front of my brother. I didn't think anything about it and went on my merry way in our fun conversation. After my brother left, I saw the look in my husband's eyes and knew something was terribly wrong. He was hurt. And I had done the hurting. He very gently, yet very strongly expressed how much he didn't like that, and how it made him feel. It was an eye-opening moment for me. We promised each other that we would always cover each other's hearts, and I had uncovered him already.

The question of how we respond to each other's weaknesses is paramount. How I respond will either cultivate intimacy, trust, passion, love, friendship, or it will break down, tear apart, weaken, and chip away at the love we promised to protect.

Love covers. Plain and simple.

There are a million moments of decision in our marriages. A million choices to make every single day, and these choices will bear fruit — either positively or negatively.

If I disrespect him or embarrass him, his heart will pull away. If I cover him, guard him, cherish him, his heart will rest in mine.

If I make room for suspicion or accusation, I will create distance, fear, or defensiveness. If I choose to believe the best in him, communicate trust and confidence, he will draw near with an open heart. If I shame him, or roll my eyes, or expose his broken places it will affect us both deeply. If I relate to him, connect with him, highlight the beauty in who he is, I will find what my heart is truly longing for.

Is he safe in my love? Does his heart rest in my presence, knowing that he - and all of his broken places - are secure?

Learning to love each other in deep authenticity has been the most transformative journey of our lives.

Growing in love for each other day by day, in the full light of honesty, has changed me forever.

Being fully seen, fully known, and still fully loved by my husband has revealed more of Christ to me than any church service ever has.

Love covers. Plain and simple.

CRAIG

How would you describe the culture of your marriage? There is one. It's unavoidable.

> *You're developing a culture in your marriage*
> *whether you realize it or not.*

Culture forms automatically. It drives the unspoken reasons why we do what we do and say what we say.

It influences our values, our tastes, our perspectives.

You have the opportunity to intentionally develop the kind of culture you desire in your marriage.

What an amazing opportunity!

In my marriage, we say certain things with great frequency:

- "I love you."
- "You're my favorite."
- "I think you're absolutely amazing."
- "I'm sorry."

- "I'm so happy you're mine."
- "You're safe with me."

Some of the things we value most are:
- authenticity,
- vulnerability,
- laughter,
- trust,
- alone time,
- date night,
- individuality.

And some things we do regularly are:
- Go on dates, long walks, laugh a lot, read together, snuggle up, exercise,
- Honor each other's alone time, play big band music while cooking, laugh easily and often,
- Choose kindness and gentleness, cheer each other on, listen well.

This (and much more) has become our culture. Our norm.

MIT professor Edgar Schein describes it like this,

> *"Culture is a way of working together toward common goals that have been followed so frequently and so successfully that people don't even think about trying to do things another way. If a culture has formed, people will autonomously do what they need to do to be successful."*[1]

It's a fun and interesting discussion to have with your spouse and one that is worth revisiting often.

What are our desires in our marriage? How do we want to move together toward those desires (say, value, do) and thus create our culture? What do we want to see and experience as the unspoken reality, atmosphere, experience in our home?

One of the things Paul was doing in his letter to the Ephesians was helping to guide healthy cultures within marriages and families (See Ephesians 5:22-6:4). He was very intentional about it. It mattered enough for him to write about it, teach into it, and highlight the right values.

He wrote to love each other, lay down your lives for each other, respect each other, sanctify each other, stay blameless towards each other, cleave to each other, nourish and cherish one another.

So very purposeful! So very powerful.

Setting your minds and hearts to build the culture you dream of is one of the best decisions you can make.

Culture will happen. One way or the other.

It's up to you.

DAY 13

CHRISTINE

My husband is an individual. I know that sounds like a no brainer, but I do forget that sometimes.

I remember the early years when I was just discovering how different we really are.

He comes from a family filled with talented actors, singers, stage-drama performers. Being in their midst is like going to a Broadway play, only better. My husband is loud. He'll talk to any stranger, about any topic (mostly Jesus), at any time. In fact, he's in the next room singing at the top of his lungs at this very moment.

I, on the other hand, have a British mother. She taught us regularly not to draw attention to ourselves. She's a humble, quiet woman who has great regard for the quietest person in the room.

My husband is an extrovert. I lean more towards being an introvert. My husband was declared an exhibitionist by a personality test. For big chunks of my life (especially in the early years)

I would fit into the painfully shy category. I remember feeling terribly embarrassed by the attention he would naturally draw. I wanted him to stop.

He should be...different.

He should be this way, or that way. He shouldn't be like that. He should definitely *not* talk to that person.

And I was wrong every single time.

I don't even know what I was thinking, to be honest. This isn't fun to admit. I think maybe I was so lacking in my own identity that everything he did somehow needed to reflect *me*. And that's a co-dependent mess!

Thankfully, it wasn't long before I began to individuate. Yes, we are one flesh. Yes, we are individuals. I believe individuating, while remaining deeply connected, is a crucial learning curve for all healthy, intimate marriages.

I am me. And he is not. And I love that about him. To truly let go and be separate, To stop should-ing all over him, Would mean celebrating his identity from the depths of my heart.

It took some practice, lots of repentance, and even more letting go. But it wasn't long before the joy of our individuality rooted deep within me.

I often shake my head in joyful wonderment, watching him across the room, completely relishing in *who* he is.

Watching him run and fly freely as I cheer him on is one of the greatest joys of my life.

I have vowed to cherish him as his own man, fully, individually, separate from me for as long as we both shall live.

CRAIG

I'm right! Aren't I?

Confession: I want to be right. I know I'm right. I'm always right! Right? Wrong. Ha!

I can't speak for you, but I think it's an inherent weakness of my humanity, this desire, this craving.

This lust for being right.

It's dangerous in a marriage, any relationship for that matter, and quite destructive.

Embarrassingly, I admit that I have often trampled on my wife's heart as I selfishly and with blind fervor raced to the top of Mount Me upon my trusty stallion, I affectionately call Ego.

And from there...grinning, wide-eyed, and self-righteously victorious, I stand alone and wonder, "Hmmm. Where's my wife? Where did she go?" And a voice replies, "Oh, your wife?

You left her at the bottom, severely wounded, alone, misunderstood...separated. And...you're alone. But, at least you're right. Right?"

What scares me about this desire, this demand that I'm right, is that it requires no love. I don't have to love to be right. But if I love, I can be wrong. I'm safe to be wrong. It's actually all right for me to be wrong. It's even expected. Because my wife knows I'm human.

Even when I forget that I am.

When I pursue being right, I always find myself standing alone.

When I pursue love,

> *I always find myself standing with her, even when I'm wrong. "Pursue love…"* (1 Corinthians 14:1, NASB)

Pursue. Love.

CHRISTINE

> *"Few are those who see with their own eyes and feel with their own hearts."* - Albert Einstein

I've heard that the opposite of love isn't hate, it's actually indifference.

I've discovered that words without heart feel hollow, empty and cold.

I've seen that affection without connection, that devotion without honesty, that action without authenticity, isn't love at all.

Learning to go through the motions is never the aim.

Approaching love with head and no heart
actually brings pain.

If your heart is disconnected, if your core has gone cold, if your head feels separate from the root of your own soul,

If your heart is disconnected, gone into hiding from the world, self-protected, distant, and afraid; if you've buried your heart from your union, from your love...

If your heart is disconnected from the spirit within, if you still go to church, worship the Lord and pray, but your heart stays distant from the Father of love, it's a serious matter. One to be tackled. For it's the intangibles that leave a wake of destruction, confusion, rejection, and shame.

> *"The Lord declares, ' This people honors me with their lips, but their heart is far from me.' "*
> (Matthew 15:8, ESV)

He also says to draw near, and He will draw near. With your whole heart, come closer.

It matters.

Treasure your heart and take it with you always.

Treasure the heart of your spouse and put connection at the top of your list. Make it a most valuable jewel.

This invisible reality, this intangible substance, this mysterious experience of heart and soul connection has the power to create — to breathe new life.

Treasure your time, your face to face moments. Cherish your glances and your eye to eye encounters.

Treasure your connection most of all,

> *"For where your treasure is, there your heart will be also."* (Matthew 6:21, NIV)

DAY 16

CRAIG

It's truly amazing and quite hard to grasp that everything in this huge universe is made up of little things like atoms.

> *"By faith we understand that the entire universe was formed at God's command, that what we now see did not come from anything that can be seen."*
> (Hebrews 11:3, NLT)

Thanks to the unseen…we have the seen. It takes the little things, the "unseen atoms" to create the big things we want to see in our marriage.

Things like love, trust, honesty, playfulness, romance, joy, friendship, comfort, connection.

They're almost imperceptible at times, but they are substantive and extremely powerful. All forming together, building upon each other, adhering and creating something beautiful to see.

These little things are as numerous as the stars.

It could be a word of encouragement, making sure not a day goes by without a hug and a kiss, or stopping what you're doing when your spouse walks into the room to be completely present.

It's the mundane things. Picking up after yourself, doing the dishes, putting gas in the car, running the errand, putting your phone down.

It's the small words. I hear you, I love you, I want only you.

It's the smallest of expressions, looking in their eyes, keeping kindness in your smile, reaching to hold their hand.

> *"Sometimes,' said Pooh, 'the smallest things take up the most room in your heart." -* A.A. Milne

Your marriage is like your own universe that God has given you to form. Your little unseen actions and thoughts; the seemingly small and simple words of love, the kindness and acceptance that emanate from *you*. All these are building blocks that are actually forming your marriage.

They're vibrating atoms obeying your commands.

Jesus told us that to the one who is faithful in the little things, much will be given.

If you want the "much" in your marriage, start with the little. One day at a time. One moment at a time.

> *"We can do no great things, only small things with great love." -* Mother Theresa

DAY 17

CHRISTINE

I wonder if some relationships fade, If some marriages fall apart, because we simply forget?

How easy it is to forget what we've promised!

We've promised to love.

To love this one person, up close and intimate, for the rest of our lives.

We've promised to love.

To lay our lives down for this one. To give ourselves to this one. To trust this one.

We've promised to love.

And this is love: (read slowly!)

> *"Love is patient, love is kind and is not jealous; love does not brag and is not arrogant, does not act unbecomingly; it does not seek its own, is not provoked, does not take into account a wrong suffered, does not rejoice in*

unrighteousness, but rejoices with the truth; bears all things, believes all things, hopes all things, endures all things. Love never fails." (1 Corinthians 13, NASB)

This scripture challenges the depths of our soul. It reveals root systems that need to be ripped up. It confronts our self-centered thinking, our worldly agendas, our immature ways.

But most of all, it disciples us, And calls us into love. The Jesus kind of love. So, I pray.... "Lord, remind me. Remind me of my promise. Remind me of love.

Don't let the world define it. Don't let the movies explain it. Don't let my fears contain it. God IS love.

Only YOU Lord, get to tell me what it looks like."

CRAIG

"One thing I ask…" - David. "One thing I do…" - Paul. "One thing is necessary…" - Jesus.

What's your one thing? Under Jesus, of course, what's your one thing as a husband?

It's a question I ponder often, because I so easily get caught up in the other things.

Those other things. My way, my opinion, my time, my feelings, my wants and desires.

I've noticed these other things often distract me from the One Thing. They bring confusion and lack of clarity. On the other hand, I've noticed that focusing on the One Thing becomes a funnel for all other things to flow through. They become washed, cleansed as it were; their value and level of importance properly revealed to me.

Purified by the hand of Love for the benefit of all.

The One Thing gives. It transmits time, attention, service, presence, grace, mercy, forgiveness, kindness; the benefit of the doubt.

The One Thing is a moment by moment offering, a surrendering of all the other things that scream for attention and declare their perceived top priority.

And please keep in mind, the other things aren't necessarily bad, they're just powerless and potentially destructive if not tempered by the One Thing.

This love that must love.

This preoccupying compulsion that demands love be first. I think that's the One Thing.

> *"For it is Christ's love that fuels our passion and motivates us."* (2 Corinthians 5:14, TPT).

And this One Thing causes all other things to have power and meaning.

And this One Thing begins with first sitting at His feet, surrendering.

Jesus told busy, preoccupied Martha that Mary had discovered the one thing most important by choosing to sit at His feet.

> *"She is undistracted, and I won't take this privilege from her."* (Luke 10:4, TPT)

And I have a hunch that later Mary lent a hand to Martha, but with a less distracted mind and a full heart.

CHRISTINE

Belonging.

It seems to be a raw human need.

People will always yearn for it, hunt it down, and even create false systems for themselves in order to find it.

This nearly desperate need to belong draws some into gangs, others into politics, cults, clubs, lodges, and tribes. It exists in every culture and every people group around the world.

The need is guttural, emotional, identity-forming, and sometimes desperate.

As Christ followers, we hope to find our belonging in His name, His love, His body, His family. We earnestly search for a community to belong to. This is right and good.

But do we look to our marriages? Do we find belonging with the one we promised to share life with?

Other than Christ Himself, my belonging is rooted in the heart of my husband.

On this Earth I am his, and his alone.

My husband has captured my heart, and I will not take it back.

My husband has a hold on me, and it's perfect. I give myself to him as completely as I know how.

I have chosen, over and over again, to find my home, my safe place, my belonging inside of this marriage.... within his love.

Sometimes I have felt the temptation to build walls.

Sometimes I can feel myself wanting to pull back, self-protect, or rest in the compromise of shallow waters.

My battle is within my own soul, and my battle is to make this a no-walls-allowed relationship. The enemy is the distance between us.

My warfare is remembering where I belong.

When I feel the ground beneath my feet shake, When my emotions feel like an unanchored kite, when fear slaps me in the face, or insecurity tries to take hold...

I remind my soul that I belong to something real, something deep, something truly spiritual and life transforming.

So much so that we share the same name, the same promise, and the same love.

> *"If we have no peace it is because we've forgotten that we belong to each other."* - Mother Teresa

CRAIG

To look means to purposefully turn towards...to see.

This is one of the many things Love does. It looks. It's always looking. Hunting, seeking, examining, studying, highlighting, gazing.

I think it's one of Love's favorite things to do... just look. Love looks.

For what? The best. Love looks for the best.

It finds it, too.

And then... believes. Love believes the best.

Even when the world seems to highlight the worst. Especially when the one you love only sees the worst in themselves.

That's a lonely, vulnerable, scary place to be, that place called Worst and all of its negative inhabitants.

But here you are married to this amazing woman, and in your promise to love this person like no other, you get to look for and believe the best.

It's a practice, for sure. It can take some time too, like hacking through a jungle.

And most of that jungle is in your own mind. Judgements, expectations, "should have's", etc. that cloud your perception.

But just keep looking. Zero in. Don't stop looking.

The invitation by God to look proves that the best is really there. It's always there.

And in the looking, in the believing, in the finding, you shelter.

You create a safe place. Void of judgment, criticism and rejection.

In fact, you *become* a safe place, a shelter in the storm. One that your wife can run to and be safe.

You become a place that declares, "Your value is beyond estimation! I love everything about you, quirks and all. I look at you now, and what I see is the best, what I see is Christ in you." What a safe place to be.

> *"Love is a safe place of shelter, for it never stops believing the best for others."* (1 Corinthians 13:7, TPT)

DAY 21

CHRISTINE

I think one of the most powerful things we could ever do is laugh. Really. No... seriously. Laughter has the power to alter the fabric of our soul and seed our relationships with life.

I'm utterly convinced.

Laughter lifts burdens that are both real and imaginary. It lightens our hearts and soothes our pains.

Laughter shifts atmospheres almost instantaneously, and causes heaviness to flee.

Laughter seems to hunt down the confident places within us, and bring them to the surface.

It carries people into joy and has a strange power to unite them together, even for a moment. I've watched a room full of strangers suddenly become connected in their humanity through laughter. I've stood in wonder as a room full of tension and division dissolved into warmth, through laughter.

I've seen laughter flow between husband and wife with an

intimate glance... a glance of shared lives, shared stories, and celebrated victories.

In marriage laughter is so deeply transformative. It has the power to create and mold the culture we dream of. A culture that gives life to freedom, trust, and ease — lifting pressure, and calming fears.

My husband and I have broken out laughing in the middle of arguments, on the heels of a deep kiss, while paying bills, cleaning house, disciplining our children.

Laughter weaves through our entire life, every single day.

Even through his battle with the darkness of depression, we could always find something to laugh about. Somehow laughter brings us together. It connects us in such a profound way, and pulls things back into perspective.

Some things will make it to the other side, some things are eternal. Marriage may not be found in heaven, but laughter will be.

Maybe letting go of illusions we hold onto, and surrendering to a good laugh is what we all need. I honestly believe it can deliver us from oppression, break the bond of deception, and send anger away confused.

As Mark Twain said: "Against the assault of laughter, nothing can stand."[2]

I wonder if laughter finds room to breathe when our hearts get a glimmer of God's majesty. If we could step out of our small world for just a moment, and remember eternity. If we can let go of the temporal and see from above, I'm sure we can find something to chuckle to about!

When we laugh together we rest in the friendship of our marriage and simply enjoy being together.

When we laugh together we find the cherish-able, and create a space in our day that feels holy.

As the old Jewish proverb says;
"As soap is to the body, so laughter is to the soul."
Laugh. Often. Together.

Amen

DAY 22

CRAIG

> *"Your love, LORD, reaches to the heavens..."*
> (Psalm 36:5, NIV)

This love that is in you by the Holy Spirit is elastic. It stretches, reaches, goes beyond. It extends itself. It can't help it.

Love reaches and it longs to touch. It *must* touch.

Love is compelled to reach for, reach into, touch, and transform. Marriage is a commitment to reaching and touching with love. That's what the love inside of you is designed to do.

God's constant invitation for us is to be stretched beyond our limits and into His limitlessness.

His limitless Love.

This kind of love reaches, stretches, beyond earthly boundaries. I think that's why it can sometimes hurt.

As St. Augustine so beautifully penned: "The measure of love, is to love without measure."

This love that is in you by the Holy Spirit has a destination. It reaches to the "heavens."

It *finds* the "heavens" inside of the other.

This love stretches and uncovers the heavenly kingdom that is within your wife. It hunts for and discovers the treasure, especially when that treasure, from time to time, might seem completely hidden.

It *refuses* to stop reaching. Even when the loving is found to be difficult.

That's the kind of love that Jesus really celebrates.

It's the kind of love I experienced from my wife when she discovered that I was abusing alcohol and lying to her about it.

She reached…and forgave.

She loved me with manifested mercy and grace, through her pain.

It wasn't easy, and it wasn't instantaneous.

But her love eventually reached to the heavens *for* me. Her love reached and found the heavens *in* me.

The love in you has a destination.

And this love will always find the heavens.

DAY 23

CHRISTINE

I'll never forget it. We were in the psychiatrist's office, following hours of testing. Craig had been deeply depressed, near suicidal for about three years. It was time to get him evaluated to see if there were other mental illnesses in the mix.

I was terrified.

In this particular meeting, the psychiatrist whipped his wheeled office chair face to face with me, leaned in closely and said "Your husband is seriously, clinically depressed. This is no small matter. You need help." He then put him on the same medicine that was used for schizophrenia.

My world was spinning.

At this point I couldn't pretend it wasn't as bad as I thought. I could no longer wash it under the rug and blame it on current, temporary circumstances. I lost the ability to gloss things over and make it all o.k.

The husband I used to have was nowhere in sight. This shell of a man, angry, faithless, dark, and hopeless was wearing the ring I put on his finger all those years ago. And I wasn't sure I even knew him anymore. He was a dark mystery. And my new reality.

I had to face the facts in front of me. And then decide.

I took some time, and gave myself permission to think scary thoughts. But I couldn't get past Jesus.

How can I follow this Jesus and think I was justified in walking away? How can I lay my life before the cross, receive its radical grace and forgiveness, scandalous, unjustified love poured out for me..... and judge my marriage unworthy of my weak love?

Jesus loved me while I was in darkness. He reached out, He pursued, He cleansed.

He still loves me, searches me out and finds me in my mess. He still dwells inside of me, no matter what. He redeems me every day.

How can I follow *this* Jesus, and justify a different kind of love? How can I stand undone by the unconditional love of my Savior in worship on Sunday and turn around and offer less to the man I've promised 'till death do us part?'

I will choose him again. Right now. In this new season. In his current state. In every new season. No matter what the cost. No matter what the trial. He is mine, and I am his.

> *"To be loved but not known is comforting but superficial. To be known and not loved is our greatest fear. But to be fully known and truly loved is, well, a lot like being loved by God. It is what we need more than anything. It liberates us from pretense, humbles us out of our self-righteousness, and fortifies us for any difficulty life can throw at us."* [3] - Timothy Keller

This is the gospel. This is marriage.

Craig was healed of his depression in 2008, ten years after it began.

Choosing to love him again, over and over again, led me to Jesus.

It was me that was redeemed, in my weak and frail love. My husband's darkness revealed my own darkness, and formed me in ways that's hard to describe.

My husband's sickness taught me how to love. In fact, my motto became "I'm just one broken person, learning how to love another broken person, regularly undone by the scandalous grace and unconditional Love of the cross."

DAY 24

CRAIG

You know that feeling when you think you've solved a mystery only to find out later that you haven't at all? And then, all of a sudden, the mystery that once appeared small and obvious is now bigger than ever and even more complex.

When you married, you entered into a mystery.

> *"Marriage is the beautiful design of the Almighty, a great and sacred mystery meant to be a vivid example of Christ and His church."* (Ephesians 5:32, TPT)

The moment we feel we have our wife figured out, when we declare the mystery solved, there's almost a smugness to it.

We relax our discernment, retire our sense of wonder, and cloak ourselves with the illusion of having full and complete knowledge of that wondrous person, even though that person (and you) are "so mysteriously complex!" (Psalm 139:14, TPT)

What if we stop trying to solve the mystery and just enter into it? What if we enter into it like a child playing Hide-and-Seek? Truthfully, when we embrace and celebrate the mystery, we can find great fun in *not* knowing. We get to hunt for clues, stumble across compelling evidence, and dust for Divine fingerprints.

As married men we've entered into a mystery with a mysterious person.... this wife of yours is your personal adventure.

Embrace it with childlike wonder! And in the midst of all the highs and lows that happen along the way, the Spirit of Love will take and use every moment to draw you ever deeper into a wondrous love. The mystery of this woman, of this love, is what compelled you at the beginning.

Decide to discover something new about your spouse as often as you can. It's easy to become lazy in our pursuit and take on a subtle indifference towards our spouse, due to familiarity.

So ask God to open your eyes in wonder towards the love of your life! Decide to watch your spouse with a keen interest; listen more, ask more questions.

And embrace the mystery.

DAY 25

CHRISTINE

> *"What we don't know about ourselves can and will hurt*
> *us, not to mention others. As long as we stay in the dark*
> *about how we see the world and the wounds and beliefs*
> *that have shaped who we are, we're prisoners of our*
> *history. We'll continue going through life on autopilot*
> *doing things that hurt and confuse ourselves and*
> *everyone around us. Eventually we become so accustomed*
> *to making the same mistakes over and over in our lives*
> *that they lull us to sleep. We need to wake up."*[4]
> - Ian Cron, *The Road Back to You*

The self aware person knows their own strengths and weaknesses well enough to steward their soul with wisdom.

The self aware person knows their own wounding well enough to seek healing, and respond well to the lies coming from that familiar pit.

The self aware person takes ownership of their own triggers, their own flaws, weaknesses and issues, and takes the steps needed for growth and healing.

A key requirement in a healthy marriage is two people agreeing to embark on the life long journey towards maturity, health, wholeness, and ownership. All of these require self awareness. Not self obsession, but responsible stewardship of your inner person.

A prideful man cannot be self aware. A prideful woman sits comfortably in her false self, leaving damaged hearts in her wake. A humble man is aware of his weaknesses, and seeks help.

A humble woman can confess her false motives, repent, and seek growth. I believe every healthy marriage needs counseling at some point in time. We can't do this alone. To think that a deep, rich marriage will 'just happen' is ludicrous.

I've heard many people say that marriage is hard work. Loving my husband is the easy part. The hard work is within my own immature soul.

The hard work is this: There is no union without surrender. There is no intimacy without humility. There is no nearness in pride. There is no love in defensiveness, arrogance, justification, un-forgiveness, offense, selfish ambition, etc.

The hard work is in my own heart. The hard work is within you. And to begin, you must know-thyself.

"To know oneself is, above all, to know what one lacks. It is to measure oneself against truth, and not the other way around. The first product of self-knowledge is humility," [5] - Flannery O'Conner

DAY 26

CRAIG

While hosting my radio show one morning I answered the phone to a loud, "I'm offended!" Making no room for me to respond, she let it fly. And, after exhausting her opinion and her verbal arsenal ran out, I simply replied. "Why are you choosing this?"

She said, "What!?"

I said, "Why are you choosing to be offended?" She went silent for a moment.

Offense is a choice. When someone declares in some form or fashion, "I take offense!" I think to myself, "Why did you bother taking it in the first place? Leave it alone and take something else."

What is it in me that thinks I can even be offended in the first place?

Am I that superior? Am I so intellectually profound and just plain awesome that all, especially my wife, must come into agreement with my ways, thoughts and desires?

And if not? I TAKE OFFENSE! I think it's a self-centered, lazy way to say,

"I disagree. I don't understand. What you said hurt me and I need to talk to you about it."

As I proceeded to discuss with that listener that offense is a choice, what we found out is that she disagreed with something I had said. Good. She didn't like what I had said. Fine.

And she took it personally due to some wounding that took place in the past. I can understand that.

But offense is the chicken way out.

What the Lord invites us into, what love calls us into, is engaging the difficult conversations healthily.

This means embarking on a learning journey, because healthy, difficult conversations don't just happen. It's a learned skill. It takes practice.

And it's a choice.

By the way, the listener ended up chuckling with me by the end of our conversation as we both realized just how funny we humans can be.

"Love is not easily irritated or quick to take offense."
(1 Corinthians 13:5, TPT)

DAY 27

CHRISTINE

I don't think any of you would disagree with the notion that our society and its culture has a twisted and often perverted view of sex. To think that we live in this particular culture, confronted by its sexual dogma at every turn, and not be affected by its perspectives, would be silly.

Many couples I've spoken to on this topic have minimized their sex life to lust, physical need and self gratification. Many couples I've spoken to on this topic have given up on sex all together. The percentages of sex-less marriages are on the rise. The percentages of Christian couples who have a difficult sex life are staggering, and it's a huge source of deep guttural pain.

This is a topic that we, as the Church, must address.

Listen to what Paul states here: Do you not know that your bodies are members of Christ? Shall I then take away the members of Christ and make them members of a prostitute? May it never be! Or do you not know that the one who joins himself to a prostitute is one body with her? For He says,

> *'The two shall become one flesh.' But the one who joins himself to the Lord is one spirit with Him."*
> (1 Corinthians 6:16-17, NASB)

Paul speaks of "one flesh" in such a way that it is clearly not just about two bodies becoming intertwined. He didn't just say that it's wrong to be with a prostitute. He said it's wrong *because* our bodies are members of Christ and our marriages are to be a synonym of our "one flesh, one spirit" relationship with the Lord. He directly compares this profound act of sex to the sacredness of our union with Christ.

He's saying that making love to someone is so deeply unifying it engages and encompasses your entire person— heart, soul, personality, emotions, spirit. And this is why Paul says it would be appalling to give yourself physically to someone that you do not have this intimacy with.

How different is this to our present day culture! It's radically antithetical to the world we live in.

Praying for revelation on God's true intention concerning man and woman's most intimate act, may just be the most important prayer you can pray for your marriage. God instigated this amazing gift for marriages. It was His idea. He created us for such deep passion. Such a profound hunger for intimacy, that words do not suffice.

God gave us this intense love that compels us towards each other, fills us with a desire for such closeness that we long to be interwoven and joined fully.

God is love. And He put within us a love that literally unites. His original design for sex is so much better than anything this world has to offer. I'm convinced that if we could get even a small glimpse of this revelation we would laugh out loud at the enemy's distortions.

So let's fight for complete redemption. Let's agree together, as husbands and wives, to never give up on our hunger to know the original. Let's not settle for the puny little perverted counterfeit of this world. Let's reach, let's pray, let's explore the ecstatic holiness of this oneness. It's worth it.

CRAIG

It's one of the most powerful weapons we have at our disposal.

Simple, yet often difficult to employ. Light weight, but can feel heavy.

Powerful enough to prevent a landslide of heartache and pain. Gentle enough to diffuse potentially volatile situations. It's peaceful, guiding, directing. And it makes… space. It creates room, lots of room for wisdom to walk in.

This weapon of ours is… The Pause. Just…pause.

Practice it in normal conversation when both parties are in agreement and all seems well.

Pause.

Pause to listen to your spouse's voice. Pause to listen to The Fathers voice. Pause to listen to what's in your own heart, for some things may not even need to be voiced.

Oh, those moments I wish I would have paused! All the heartache that would have been avoided.

Pausing can feel like a waste of time, but in reality you're suspending time. You're holding that moment open, taking a breath, and giving room for the Holy Spirit to make it a sacred space.

And He will shape it. Because that's what He does. And He'll direct it into a pathway of peace.

A simple pause creates space for wisdom, understanding and love to have their say. It diffuses our reactions, our triggers, our selfish impulses. It just takes a moment to silence the flesh and cultivate space. The Holy Spirit is drawn to empty spaces. Remember, He creates in the void.

So practice the pause.

When needed, you will be ready to wield this unassuming weapon.

> *"Be quick to listen, but slow to speak. And be slow to become angry."* (James 1:19, TPT)

DAY 29

CHRISTINE

Ephesians 5:21 says, "...and be subject to one another in reverence of Christ."

Being subject means servanthood, submission, to rank under, to obey. It's a bowing low of our will, letting go of our pride, willingly, joyfully serving and following the other.

Both. Mutual. Two hearts, bowing low... to one another.

My favorite part of this scripture is the phrase "in reverence of Christ."

I will lay myself low, *because* I stand in awe of Jesus. I will joyfully be led, *because* I still tremble when He speaks. We will serve, we will submit to each other, because our hearts are caught in the captivating, majestic presence of the Holy One.

When we are both drenched in the awe and wonder of our King, mutual submission flows joyfully.

We can't do anything without Him.

The Ephesians passage on marriage begins with an extensive paragraph on being filled with the Holy Spirit. The power of this anointed union between husband and wife gets to be displayed to the world, as a sign and wonder, pointing to the King of Kings.

Your marriage, bottom line, is called to be a supernatural move of the Holy Spirit.

Rely on Him, and He will fill you. Lean on Him, and He will empower you. Draw close to Him, and He will anoint you for love. Stand in awe of the King, in reverence to the Holy One, and you will find that your submission to each other will be one of your greatest acts of worship.

CRAIG

Remain eager. Earnestly endeavor. Run swiftly. Press on.

These are all ways to describe what it is to pursue love.

What makes action/adventure or romantic movies so fun and exciting? The pursuit! The car chases and runs on rooftops; the tracking down, the close calls of apprehension, missed phone calls, and those "just in the nick of time" encounters.

We men love the pursuit. We were designed to pursue because we were designed for love.

And …. love pursues.

"Pursue love…" (1 Corinthians 14:1, ESV) But, how? *How* do we pursue love? By loving. By seeking her heart. Over and over again. The pursuit is in the giving. The focus. The offering of your heart. The pursuit is in the loving.

God is love. He pursued you. And now you pursue Him.

You can't truly love and *not* pursue.

Giving love *is* pursuing love.

In marriage we get to do what God did. We initiate the pursuit.

When you remain eager to love your wife through thick and thin, when you earnestly endeavor to love the one you chose, when something in you says run away, but you run swiftly into their heart instead. When you press on, despite problems and pain, because you are determined to love.

Then you are pursuing love.

But know this: in your own strength it's impossible. Only God can love like this.

So…

Holy Spirit has been poured within you for this very pursuit. How eager Holy Spirit is to love!

Thank God Holy Spirit presses on, no matter what, to shed abroad in our hearts the very love of God! Leading us, guiding us.

When you and I pursue love we are actually pursuing something that's pursuing us.

And in your marriage you get to partner with Holy Spirit in this crazy pursuit. It's like that moment in the midst of a chase when you run right into the other person in an alleyway and realize you both have been pursuing each other all along.

Your wedding day was not the end of the pursuit. It was the beginning of many pursuits!

The chase is on. It's always on.

CRAIG AND CHRISTINE

One more thing. Have fun! Together, that is. Have fun *together*.

> *"Seriousness is too boring to the playful human*
> *condition. A heart of stone that has a long face*
> *can never express love."*[6] - Michael Bassey Johnson

Can you imagine what Adam and Eve experienced in the Garden before the fall? Many things for sure, but among those, you *know* it had to be fun!

God told Abraham that He would establish His everlasting covenant with Isaac. Isaac means 'to laugh' and comes from a root word that means 'play'. Just think. God establishing His love, His promise, on laughter and play!

Let Jesus look at you with a wink and say, "You two are in love! How do you want to celebrate that today?"

It's far too easy to minimize the importance of fun. Some people think fun just happens accidentally sometimes. Some people think it's frivolous. And some others hardly ever think about it at all.

God's covenant was established on laughter and play. It's important.

In Proverbs 8:30-31 we see this picture of Jesus, as Wisdom, at the beginning of creation, rejoicing and taking delight in the sons of men. The word "rejoicing" in Hebrew literally means "laughing and playing."

That means that as the Lord Himself was breathing life into the human race, it was *fun*.

We are made for joy. We are hard-wired for laughter. We were created in an atmosphere of fun.

Every love affair needs fun to survive. It's as necessary as oxygen.

But fun usually needs a little planning.

So make it one of your disciplines. Keep it as one of your values. Hold it as a priority.

And always remember:
Sometimes having fun with your best friend
is all the therapy you need.

NOTES

1   Schein, Edgar. McKay, Brett & Kate. "Fathering with
Intentionality: The Importance of Creating a Family Culture."
The Art of Manliness, 20 July 2022, https://www.artofmanliness.
com/people/fatherhood/family-culture/.

2   Twain, Mark. T*he Mysterious Stranger and Other Curious Tales.*
Gramercy Books, 1997.

3   Keller, Timothy, and Kathy Keller. *The Meaning of Marriage:
Facing the Complexities of Commitment with the Wisdom of God.*
Penguin Books, 2016.

4   Cron, Ian Morgan. *The Road Back to You: An Enneagram
Journey to Self-Discovery.* IVP Books, an Imprint of InterVarsity
Press, 2016.

5   O'Connor, Flannery, and Sally Fitzgerald. *Mystery and
Manners Occasional Prose.* Farrar, Straus & Giroux, 1969.

6   Johnson, Michael Bassey. *The Infinity Sign.* Independently
Published, 2015.

Printed in Great Britain
by Amazon

20095764R00048